GIGGLES & SLAPPER

Copyright © 2020 Giggles & Slapper
All rights reserved.
ISBN: 9798624220782

Other Books by
Giggles & Slapper

Jurassic Jokes:
A Joke Book 65 Million Years in the Making

The Geektastic Joke Book 4 Kids
An unofficial collection of Pop Culture funniness

This book is unofficial and unauthorized. It is a work of parody and is not approved, licensed, authorized or endorsed by Lucas Films, The Walt Disney Company, George Lucas, The First Order, The Old Republic, The Jedi Council or The Empire. Anyone claiming differently should be punished by way of Order 66.

STAR WARS
THE JOKES AWAKEN

Thank you for picking up a copy of Star Wars: The Jokes Awaken, the third joke book by Giggles A. Lott and Nee Slapper. This installment will take you to a galaxy far far away as we dive into the most popular franchise on the planet Earth. Even if you have never seen a Star Wars film you can't escape the reach and pop culture influence of George Lucas's creation. So, sit back and enjoy this book full of everything from classic Star Wars jokes, cartoons, and Rebus puzzles, to new jokes paying homage to the latest installments to the franchise.

And remember, the farce will be with you always...

Giggles & Slapper

How long did Han Solo live?
All his life

What website did Chewy build to share the First Order's secrets?
Wookieleaks

What is Darth Vader's email address?
Lord Vader AT-AT gmail dot com

Why is Yoda such a good gardener?
A green thumb, he has

What would you call a movie in which Luke never tells the truth?
Star Wars: The Lies of Skywalker

What do you call a nerdy space station?
The Dork Star

What do you call the Ewok who stuck his right paw in a Rancor's mouth?
Lefty

What does Admiral Ackbar take when he is tired?
It's a *NAP!*

Star Wars: The Jokes Awaken

What is a Stormtrooper's favorite TV show?

Game of Clones

What do you call a Chicken Sith Lord?

Kylo Hen

What do you call a space container with the power to destroy a planet?

The Death Jar

Where do Sith Lords shop?

At the Darth Maul

Star Wars: The Jokes Awaken

What do you use to cook an inhabitant of Endor?
An E-Wok

Why did the episode movies come out 4, 5, 6, then 1, 2, 3?
In charge of scheduling, Yoda was

What is the internal temperature of a Tauntaun?
Lukewarm

What code name do rebel frogs use?
Toad One

Use the force to solve this Rebus Puzzle

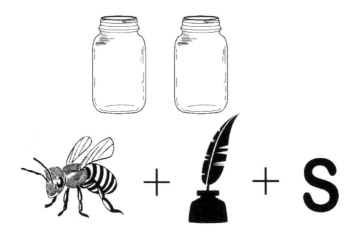

How do Wookies taste?
Chewy

What do you get if you combine a bounty hunter and a tropical fruit?
Mango Fett

What do you call a droid that wets itself?
C-3 PP-0

What did the Mandalorian say after leading his horse to a huge pile of straw?

"This is the hey"

If Jedi could get married how would they split up?

By using Di Force

What is Jabba the Hutt's middle name?

The

What do you get when you cross a Sith Lord with a country singer?

Darth Brooks

What did Obi Wan say when Luke gave him a spork?

"That's no spoon"

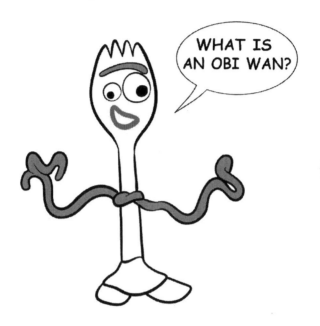

What do you call a smelly Gungan?

Jar Jar Stinks

What do you call a Mandalorian cheese?

Bobo – Fetta

How did Mace die in Star Wars?
Through the Windu

What is a Sith Lord's favorite drink at the bar?
A Palpitini

How do you wish a Jedi good luck in the south?
May the Force be with y'all

What dressing does Luke put on his porg salad?
Skywalker Ranch Lite Side Dressing

Star Wars: The Jokes Awaken

What do you call a group of small rocks that rebel against the Empire?

The Pebble Alliance

How do Tusken Raiders cheat on their taxes?

They always single file, to hide their numbers

What is the most popular coffee shop on Tatooine?

Java the Hutt

If you get your hand cut off by a lightsaber, where should you go to get a new one?

A second hand store

Why can't you email a photo to a Jedi?

Because attachments are forbidden

What do you call a Jedi without an eye?

Jed

Jabba the Hutt is so fat...

Jabba the Hutt is so fat when he sat on his iPhone he turned it into an iPad.

Jabba the Hutt is so fat when he sits around the Palace, he sits next to everybody.

Jabba the Hutt is so fat you have to take two landspeeders just to get on his good side.

Jabba the Hutt is so fat he has more rolls than a bakery.

Jabba the Hutt is so fat Obi Wan looked at him and said, "That's no moon."

Jabba the Hutt is so fat that his belly-button's got an echo!

Jabba the Hutt is so fat he is on both sides of his family tree.

What do you call five Siths piled on top of a lightsaber?

A Sith-Kabob

Why are Imperial Fighter Pilots fed up with space battles?

Because they always end up in a TIE

Where do Gungans keep their jelly?

In Jar Jars

What is Admiral Ackbar's favorite coffee drink?

It's a FRAP

MAY THE FROTH BE WITH YOU

What happens when an orange and white X-Wing crashes into green water?

It gets wet

Why did the Star Wars fan make his car look like a Stormtrooper?

So it wouldn't hit anything

Why did the Stormtrooper drop his weapon and cross the road?

Because Rey told him too

Why did the Stormtrooper call tech support for his laptop?

He had troubleshooting issues

Star Wars: The Jokes Awaken

How do you get a Stormtrooper to hit a target?

Push him into it

Why do Stormtroopers never get vaccinated?

Because they keep missing their shots

THE STORMTROOPER DARTS TEAM

What happened to the kamikaze Stormtrooper?

Nothing, he survived 99 missions

Did you hear about the band called The Stormtroopers?

They never had a hit

What do you call a pirate droid?

Argh2-D2

What is the Federation Battle Droid's favorite baseball team?

Dodger-Dodgers

DODGER DODGER

Why did the angry Jedi cross the road?

To get to the dark side

Why do Doctors make the best Jedi?

A Jedi must have patience

Why does Princess Leia keep her hair tied up in buns?

So it doesn't Hang So-low

How do you unlock doors on Kashyyyk?

With a woo-key

How do Sith Lords like their toast?
On the dark side

What do you get when you combine a silly old bear stuffed with fluff and a rebel fighter pilot?
Pooh Dameron

POOH DAMERON

What do resistance fighters chew to keep their breath fresh?
Rebel Gum

What computer language do the Hutts use?
JabbaScript

Why does Yoda sit in the same seat on the Jedi Council?
He likes to sit next to a Windu

What do you call an ugly Jedi?

DontLuke Skywalker

What Jedi uses deli meat as a weapon?
Obi Wan Baloney

What droid always goes the wrong way?
R2-Detour

What do you call an invisible protocol droid?
C-though-PO

When is a land speeder not a land speeder?
When it turns into a driveway

What did Han Solo say to the waiter who recommended the haddock?
"Never sell me the cods"

What are Sandpeople's favorite football team?

The Raiders – Tusken Raiders

What do you call a Star Wars themed all-you-can-eat restaurant?

Bo-buffet

Why does Yoda always need to borrow money?

He is a little short

What time is it when a Bantha sits on your droid?
Time to get a new droid

What do you get if you combine a potato and a Sith Lord?
Darth Tater

DARTH TATER

Where does the Emperor go to the bathroom?
In the Imperial Pooper

What do you call one hand clapping?
Hand Solo

What do you call a Clone Trooper from the Lone Star State?
Captain Tex

CAPTAIN TEX

Star Wars: The Jokes Awaken

How do X-wing fighter pilots cheat on their exams?
Copy red leader

How is Duct Tape like the Force?
It has a Dark Side, a Light side and it binds the galaxy together

Why is Darth Vader not safe for children under age 3?
He's a choking hazard!

Where do you take a sick Tauntaun?
To a Hoth-pital

Star Wars: The Jokes Awaken

EXPRESSIONS OF VADER

HAPPY	SAD	PROUD
CONFUSED	MAD	SLEEPY
FRUSTRATED	EXCITED	SASSY

Why did the nerdy Jedi cross the road?

To get to the dork side

What do you call a Stormtrooper in an Ice Cream truck?

A Snow Clone

What kind of space battles do pirates have?

Starrrgh Wars

What do giant space slugs (Exogorths) take to get cleaned up?

Meteor Showers

Why wasn't the droid hungry?

Because BB-8

How long has Anakin Skywalker been evil?
Since the Sith Grade

What do you call a rebel princess who only shops at Whole Foods?
Leia Organic

What do Rebels eat when they need a quick bite?
An Admiral Snack Bar

Yoda is so old...

Yoda is so old, he walked into an antique store and they sold him.

Yoda is so old, his birth certificate expired.

Yoda is so old that if he acted his age, he'd drop dead.

Star Wars: The Jokes Awaken

Yoda is so old when he went to school there was no history class.

Yoda is so old his memory is in black and white.

What did Palpatine say to Vader during the holidays?

Merry Sithmas

How did Vader know what Luke was getting him for Christmas?

He felt his presents

What's Boba Fett's favorite Christmas song?

Jango bells, Jango bells, Jango all the way...

What do you call a Zombie Ewok?

The Ewoking Dead

What do you call an Ewok that refuses to go outside?

An Endor Ewok

Why did the Millennium Falcon get a ticket?

Chewy forgot to pay the parking meteor

What do you get when you combine a Clone Trooper with a Dinosaur?

Captain T-Rex

CAPTAIN T-REX

What is Yoda's favorite dinosaur?

The Do-ceratops, there is no tri

Star Wars: The Jokes Awaken

Why are Supreme Leader Snokes and Darth Mauls such great deals?

Because they are half off

Why did the tiniest Jedi in the universe cross the road?

He was riding the chicken

What do First Order Troops like to have with their pizza?

Cheesy Sticks and Dreadnoughts

What Star Wars character brings you food?
Darth Waiter

What do you call a Sith that runs away from a fight?
A Sithy

Star Wars: The Jokes Awaken

Use the force to solve this Rebus Puzzle

Oh + 🐝 + ✨/ − d

🥫 + oh + 🐝

Did you know that a Rancor can jump higher than a house?
Its true because a house can't jump at all

Why does Supreme Leader Snoke always beat everyone to the restaurant?
Because he likes to get in the First Order

How do you stop Baby Yoda from throwing a tantrum?

You say, Do or Do not, there is no Cry

What kind of car does a jedi drive?

A Toy Yoda

When did Baby Yoda say his first word?

Right after his second word

What is the real reason the Mandalorian does not take off his helmet?

Baby Yoda's full dipper

What is General Dameron's favorite kind of sandwich?

A Po Boy

What is Admiral Ackbar's favorite kind of sandwich?

It's a WRAP!

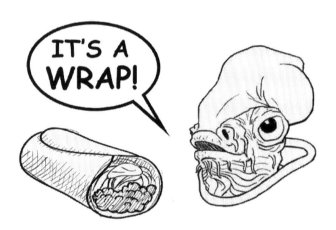

What did Obi Wan say to Luke when he tried to eat bantha pie with a spoon?

Use the fork, Luke

What do Whiphids say when they kiss?
Ouch!

What side of Yoda is the most wrinkled?
The outside

How many Jedi does it take to screw in a light bulb?
None. They have their padawan do it

What do you get when you combine a flightless bird and a droid?

A Cy-porg

CYPORG

How do Ewoks communicate over long distances?
Ewokie Talkies

What kind of tea do Mandalorians drink?
Boba

Which soldiers in Star Wars smell the best?
The Cologne Troopers

Which Jedi was the most nervous?
Panakin Skywalker

When a Problem Comes Along, You Must Wicket

WICKET GOOD!

What is the name of Darth Vader's sister, whose career in the Empire went up and down?

Ellie Vader

What do Winnie the Pooh and Jabba the Hutt have in common?

The same middle name

What position do Jawas usually play in baseball?

Short Stop

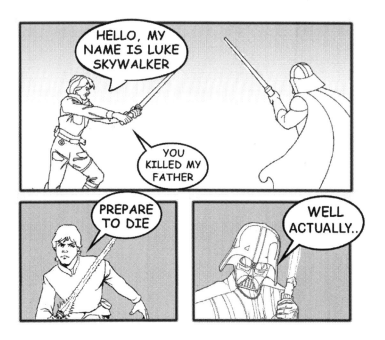

If Rob Reiner directed The Empire Strikes Back

What do you call the person that brings dinner to a Rancor?
The appetizer

What do you do with a blue Rancor?
Cheer it up

What do Rancors have that no other creature in the galaxy has?
Baby Rancors

MOVIE MASHUP

What side of a Tauntaun is the warmest?
The Inside

Why did Darth Vader search the guitar shop?
To find the hidden rebel bass

How many Sith does it take to change a light bulb?
None. They like it on the dark side

What is Darth Vader's favorite Disney song?
When You Wish Upon A Death Star

How did the fat resistance fighter get into his X-wing?
He'd Wedge himself in

What do you call a Gungan in the third grade?
A Yungan

Star Wars: The Jokes Awaken

Why doesn't Yoda have body odor?

He wears De-Yoda-Rant

Why is the Imperial Fleet like a gossip magazine?

Its full of Star Destroyers

How did Darth Vader cheat at Poker?

He kept altering the deal

What's a Jawa's favorite vegetable?
Zucchini

What does Kylo Ren serve at a dinner party?
First hors d'oeuvres

What Sith name did the galaxy's ugliest man get when he joined the dark side?
Darth Hideous

Darth Hideous is so ugly...

Darth Hideous is so ugly that when he cries the tears run down the back of his head because they are afraid of his face

Darth Hideous is so ugly, when he was born the doctor slapped his parents!

Darth Hideous is so ugly when he walks into a bank, they turn off the security cameras.

Darth Hideous is so ugly, when he looks in the mirror, the reflection ducks!

Knock Knock

Who's there

Yoda

Yoda who?

Yoda-Lay-Hee-Hoo

Knock Knock

Who's there?

Amidala

Amidala who?

Amidala short, can you lend me some money?

Knock knock.

Who's there?

Dook.

Dook-who?

Count Dook-who

What is Kylo Ren's favorite kind of coffee?

Dark Roast

After eating a plate of cookies, what did Poe, Rey, and Finn leave all over the table?

Rebel Crumbs

SPIDER-MAN vs. THE WALKING THINGIES

What happens when Jar Jar gets something in his eye?
Jar Jar Blinks

Why were Uncle Owen and Aunt Beru such good farmers?
They tried their harvest

What do you call a small cut or wound you get on Padmé Amidala's home planet?

A Naboo-boo

Why are droid mechanics never lonely?

Because they can build new friends

When does a Rancor catch a bus?

When it is thrown at them

What do Stormtroopers get if they play with space frogs?

What do star destroyers wear to parties
Bo TIEs

What did one lightsaber say to the other lightsaber?
Nothing. Lightsabers don't talk

What is Obi Wan's favorite cereal?
Jedi Mind Trix

What's the best dance club in the First Order?

Why don't Ewoks pee in the woods?
Because they have Endor Pluming

What goes ha ha ha ha clunk?
A droid laughing his head off

Why did Darth Maul's restaurant in space fail?
It had no atmosphere

What is scarier than a charging platoon of Stormtroopers?
The Ewoks chasing them

Why don't Porgs trust the ocean?

It smells a little fishy

What do you get when you cross a Jedi weapon and a prehistoric cat?

A Light Saber-Toothed Tiger

Who is Aquaman's new favorite Star Wars character?

Finn

Why did the Ewoks cross the road?

They were chasing Stormtroopers

How do you make a Rathtar laugh?

With ten-tickles

What should you do if a Rancor swallows you whole?

Run around until you're all pooped out

What two things does a Rancor never eat for Lunch?

Breakfast and Dinner

Where do Wampas keep their money?

In snow banks

What always follows a Tauntaun?

Their tail

How do you stop a Rathtar from charging?

Take away its credit card

How many Snowspeeders can you put in an empty hanger?

Just one. After the first Snowspeeder is in the hanger it isn't empty anymore

How many stars are in the universe?

All of them

What do you say to a dead droid?

Rust in piece

When can three Tauntauns be under one umbrella and not get wet?

When it's not raining

Want some BIG dinosaur-sized laughs?

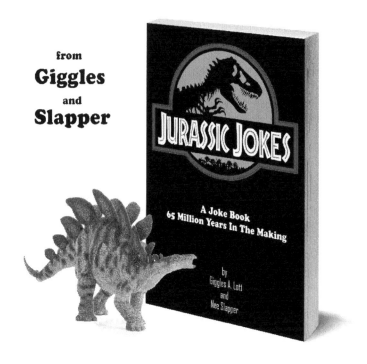

JURASSIC JOKES: *A Joke Book 65 Million Years in the Making!*

Giggles & Slapper have done it again in their second Joke Book for kids dedicated to all things dinosaur and prehistoric.

Available at: AMAZON and Barnes & Noble.com in Paperback and e-book

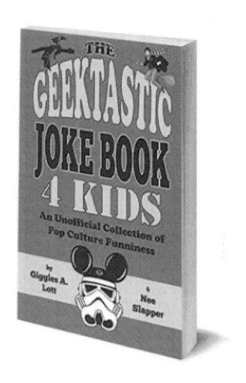

*Keep the laughs going wth
Giggles & Slapper's*
THE GEEKTASTIC JOKE BOOK 4 KIDS

A collection of the best jokes about Star Wars, Disney, Superheroes, Minecraft, Monsters, the world of Harry Potter, Video Games, Dinosaurs, Doctor Who, Star Trek, The Hunger Games and so much more!

Available at: AMAZON and Barnes & Noble.com in Paperback and e-book

Night of the Zom*BEE*s
A Zombie novel with real BUZZ!

Some laughs and some scares in this YA (ages 12 and up) horror comedy adventure with plenty of twists and turns. Follow three reluctant teens as they fight their way through the undead and try to save their hometown before its overrun by *ZomBEEs*.

Available at: AMAZON and Barnes & Noble.com in Paperback, e-book, and audiobook

Also available at Amazon,
Barnes & Noble.com
Supernatural Comedy Horror (Ages 15 plus)

Night of the Living Trekkies
by Kevin David Anderson & Sam Stall

Midnight Men
The Supernatural Adventures of Earl and Dale
by Kevin David Anderson

Made in the USA
Middletown, DE
28 November 2020